The Catholic Church of England.

Its
Constitution, Faith, Episcopal Succession, etc.

Published by
Direction of the Archbishop and to be obtained from
The Secretary,
5, Ethelbert Road, Bromley, Ken.
============
Price One Shilling Sixpence

Copyright © 2015 by St. Gabriel Theological Press. All Rights Reserved.

No part of this publication may be reproduced, distributed, or transmitted in any form or by any means, including photocopying, recording, or other electronic and mechanical methods, without the prior written permission of the publisher, except in case of brief quotations embodied for critical reviews and certain noncommercial uses permitted by copyright law.

ISBN: 978-1-329-56792-4

The ..
Catholic Church of England
Ancient, Western and Orthodox,
In the Patriarchate of Old Rome,
Known, Therefore, as Old Roman Catholic.

THE Hierarchy was restored to England by the old Roman Catholic Archbishop of Utrecht, 28th, April, 1908. The Catholic Church of England was united with the Orthodox Patriarchate of Antioch, by the Prince Archbishop of Beirut, 5th August, 1911. . . . .

Notice to the Bishops and Clergy the Catholic Church of England

This publication is to be regarded by our Bishops and Clergy as authorative, and as binding upon all who are united with us.

+ Arnold Harris Mathew.
Archbishop and Metropolitan of the London District

ASCENSION DAY, 1914.

Introduction
Most Reverend William Myers

This work was first published by Archbishop Arnold Harris Mathew in 1914. It provides valuable insight into his goals and aspirations for the Old Roman Catholic Church (then called the Catholic Church of England).

When we decided to republish the work, it was determined to keep the formatting as close to the original as possible. This includes replicating fonts as closely as possible, replicating any errors, and maintaining the typesetting. Therefore, some words and styles may appear foreign to the modern reader.

I hope that this publication becomes a helpful piece for all interested in Archbishop Mathew and the movement. He has been claimed by various groups and factions throughout the history of our Church but primary sources such as this work reveal his true intention. It appears to me that his goal was to serve the people of God where possible regardless of the barriers that separate us.

This is an admirable goal and one that our Church continues to attempt to replicate. May God bless our little part of the Church and all who receive our ministrations.

+William Myers
9/21/2015

The..
Catholic Church of England.
Ancient, Western and Orthodox,
And in the Patriarchate of Rome.

I. – CONSTITUTION

1. The Catholic Church of England follows the apostolic custom of election to the degrees of ministry, in order that its Bishops and Priests may become ministers and servants, and not the lords and masters, of the Faithful.

2. The Catholic Church of England, like the Catholic Church in other countries, is organized as a national church, its bond of union with the whole Church everywhere being the identity of its Faith with that of the universal Church, before the lamentable division of the East from the West in 1057. Whilst upholding the same Faith as the other Catholic and Apostolic Churches, the Catholic Church of England is autonomous, and is independent of exterior control in the management of its affairs within its own province.

3. England is, for our purposes, divided into five districts, *viz.*, (1) The London District, comprising of the county of Middlesex ; (2) The Northern District, comprising of the counties of Northumberland, Cumberland, Westmorland, Durham, Lancastershire, Yorkshire, and the Isle of Man ; (3) The Eastern District, comprising of the counties of Derbyshire, Nottinghamshire, Lincolnshire, Leicestershire, Rutland, Northamptonshire, Huntingdonshire, Hertfordshire and Bedfordshire ; (4) The Western District, comprising of the whole of Wales, with the countries of Cheshire, Staffordshire, Shropshire, Warwickshire, Worcestershire, Herefordshire, Monmouthshire, Gloucester, Oxford, and Berkshire ; (5) The Southern District, comprising the counties of Cornwall, Devon, Somerset, Dorset, Hampshire, Wiltshire, Sussex, Surrey and Kent, also the Chanel Islands. London is the Metropolitan See, to which the four other Sees are Suffragan. Whenever the necessity arises, other divisions and arrangements will be made by the Episcopal Synod.

4. The Bishops will be elected by the Episcopal Synod, assisted by the clergy, who will act as representatives of their respective flocks at Episcopal elections. The elections will take place

by ballot, in the Metropolitan Church, after the celebration of the Mass *de Spiritu Sancto,* in all cases of voting there must be a majority of two-thirds to carry a motion.

5. The Bishops of the Catholic Church of England are to be regarded as presiding in their respective dioceses, and as possessing those spiritual powers which appertain to the Episcopate as especially representing our Divine Lord Himself, and therefore claiming our particular respect and obedience in spiritual things.

6. The clergy and religious orders within each district are under an obligation of canonical obedience to the Bishop of that district, with the right of appeal to the Episcopal Synod, the decision of which must be accepted as final.

Each Bishop will form a chapter of at least four and not more than ten Canons, under a Dean. The Senior Canon, after the Dean, will be the Archdeacon of his district. The clergy agree and undertake by their oath of obedience at their ordination, to perform the duties in the spheres allotted to them by their respective Bishops, and to vacate these duties, spheres of labour and the edifices, of whatever kind, attached to them, when required to do so by their respective Bishops or by the Episcopal Synod.

The Episcopal Synod is composed of the Archbishop of the London district, and all the Suffragan and Assistant Bishops, together with the Dean and Archdeacon of each Chapter.

7. The Archbishop of the London district is Metropolitan for all England. He is, however, like every other individual Bishop bound by the decrees and decisions of the Episcopal Synod, to which he must submit in the event of dispute or deposition. It is his duty always to preside at Synodical Meetings, unless prevented, when me must request the Episcopal Synod to elect a deputy. He must act as intermediary in any questions affecting relations with the State in any department. He must confirm Bishops in their Episcopal appointments, and perform the consecration of Bishops. In his absence the senior Bishop by consecration will fulfill the Archbishop's duties. It is his duty to summon provincial councils and to assemble congresses in conjunction with foreign and colonial or Irish and Scottish Metropolitans. An International Congress should be assembled annually in London, to which all representatives of the Catholic Episcopal and Orthodox Catholic Churches should be invited.

The Metropolitan must preside at Episcopal Courts convened to hear complaints against Bishops, Priests and Religious. He may address Encyclical Letters to the whole Church Catholic.

8. The Catholic Church of England, thus established in autonomy and independence, forms a part of the One Holy Catholic and Apostolic Church, of which our Divine Lord Jesus Christ is the Supreme Head.

9. The Catholic Church of England recognizes and extends the right hand of fellowship to all who hold the Catholic and Orthodox Faith. It is her desire and mission to promote union and charity among all believers in God, to extend the Faith by all legitimate means, and to lay stress upon all points of agreement which may be discovered between herself and other Christian bodies.

RULES BY WHICH THE CLERGY UNDERTAKE TO BE BOUND.

1. The clergy are under strict obligation to regard their ordination promises as binding in conscience. They undertake to remain attached to the work, or parish, entrusted to them, until removed, or permitted to go, to other spheres, by the ordinary. No one receiving ordination as a priest of the Catholic Church of England may abandon the movement in England without the formal permission of his Diocesan and that of the Metropolitan.

2. Should any priest be deposed from his cure by his Ordinary, he, in virtue of his ordination vow of obedience, is bound and agrees to vacate his position, and to surrender, to the Episcopal Chapter, possession of any buildings and Church property of any and every description of which he may have been in charge.

3. All donations of money, in kind or in real estate, made to the clergy, are to be regarded as given to them in trust for the use of the Catholic Church of England, and not as personal gifts, unless the donors expressly state, in writing, that such gifts are intended as personal presents, and not given to be devoted and to belong to the movement.

In the event of the death of any Bishop or Priest, all ecclesiastical property in his custody at the time of his decease is to be regarded as belonging to the Episcopal Chapter, and may on no account be alienated or included in the personal or real estate of the deceased, unless satisfactory evidence shall be forthcoming that it belonged to the deceased as his own legitimate personal property.

4. The Episcopal Chapter may, by a voting majority of two-thirds of the members with the Metropolitan, depose and dismiss any Bishop or Priest who may be proved to be incapable of fulfilling his duties or guilty of any act of simony or offence against morality, temperance or the civil law, or as dis-edifying in his life, example or conversation. Any ecclesiastic so deposed undertakes and is bound to submit, absolutely and without question, to the act of deposition, as soon as it shall be communicated to him by the Metropolitan, or by some other person deputed for this purpose by the Episcopal Chapter.

5. No Bishop may exercise episcopal functions outside of the district of which he is Ordinary, without the consent of the Diocesan in whose district he wishes to officiate.

No priest may exercise his sacerdotal functions outside his own parochial district, without the permission of his Ordinary, or, if it be other Episcopal Districts than his own, without the further permission of the respective Ordinaries.

6. No priest may inaugurate a new mission, or assist any layman or other person to inaugurate a new mission, without the sanction of his Diocesan, nor may any layman undertake to lecture, or to hold any public religious services in connexion with the Catholic Church of England, without the formal sanction and approval, in writing, of the Metropolitan.

7. Persons who are attached to other denominations than the Catholic Church of England are not entitled to communicate and will not be admitted to receive Holy Communion at her altars, until they have formally united with the Catholic Church of England.

8. Anglican Orders are not recognized as valid by the Catholic Church of England. Anglican clergymen uniting with that Church will receive conditional Baptism, Confirmation, the first Tonsure, the four minor Orders and the three Holy Orders. The major or Holy Orders will be given *sub conditione*.

9. The Bishops and Priests of the Catholic Church of England are not allowed to communicate at Anglican or Protestant "eucharistic" celebrations. They may, however, accept invitations to preach the Gospel in Anglican or in Protestant places of worship provided such preaching does not involve any recognition, or even *quasi*-recognition, of Anglican Orders as valid.

The above prohibitions do not apply in the case of Anglican beneficed clergymen who are known to have been validly ordained either in the Roman Catholic, or in the Oriental, or in the Old Catholic Churches, or by Bishops of the Catholic Church of England for the O. C. R.

When Anglican clergymen are known to have received valid ordination from any source outside the Anglican communion, the clergy of the Catholic Church of England may co-operate with them and officiate in their churches provided such clergymen hold all the Articles of the Faith of the Catholic Church of England, as laid down therein.

10. All priests of the Catholic Church of England and of the O. C. R. must be men of Faith and Prayer. "Take heed to yourselves and to the whole flock, wherein the Holy Ghost hath placed you Bishops,

to rule the Church of God, which He hath purchased with His own blood " (Acts, xx. 28). Without Faith it is impossible to please God, and without prayer it is impossible to preserve union with Him. No Bishop or Priest can expect his ministry to be blessed or fruitful unless he "Take heed" to himself, sanctifying his soul by daily meditation, the celebration of the holy Mass, the recitation of at least some portion of the Divine Office, or, when this is impossible, of the fifteen mysteries of the Rosary, which provide us with an easily remembered series of meditations upon the chief events in the life of our Divine Lord and of His Blessed Mother. All Bishops and Priests will remember not only to advocate but to practice examination of conscience and confession at regular intervals. "Let no man despise thy youth, but be thou and example to the faithful in word, in conversation, in charity, in faith, in chasity... Attend unto reading, to exhortation, and to doctrine" (I. Tim., iv. 12, 13).

11. The official designation of our portion of the Catholic Church shall, for the future, be "The Catholic Church of England," and in other countries the Churches in communion with us will be known as the Catholic Churches of their respective nations, *e.g.*, the Catholic Church of Ireland, the Catholic Church of Scotland, the Catholic Church of France, the Catholic Church of North America, etc., etc.

The clergy are to be careful to adopt this designation, exclusively, for the future.

REGULATIONS TO BE OBSERVED BY CLERICAL MEMBERS OF THE ORDER OF CORPORATE REUNION.

1. Those Anglican clergymen who have received valid ordination from Bishops of the Catholic Church of England, are expected to celebrate Mass daily, and to do so in accordance with all the rubrical directives contained in the *Missale Romanum*.

2. Wherever it may be possible to use the Missal, either in Latin or in the vernacular rendering, this should be done, in place of the mutilated rite sacrilegiously introduced by Cranmer and the Tudor "reformers" of the Anglican communion. Where the Missal cannot be used in public Masses, the defects of the Cranmerian rite of the Book of Common Prayer must be made good by the use of approved liturgical books.*

3. All validly ordained Anglican clergymen, who are in union with the Catholic Church of England, must use all possible diligence in ascertaining whether their parishioners have been validly baptized, and in cases where any possible doubt as to the validity of baptism exists, they must administer conditional baptism ; and no persons of whose valid Baptism doubts may exist is to be allowed to approach the Sacraments until such doubts shall have been removed.

4. No persons should be admitted to receive Holy Communion but such as have been fully and adequately instructed, but uninstructed persons may receive *pain benit*, in the manner customary in many foreign churches, as a sacramental.

5. The Anglican rite of Confirmation is invalid as a sacramental rite, and it is merely equivalent to a renewal of baptismal vows. The clergy of the Order of Corporate Reunion should, therefore, endeavour to obtain the services of a Bishop of the Catholic Church of England, or of a Bishop in valid orders of the O. C. R., to administer the sacrament of Confirmation, with the Catholic rite and the Chrism, to all instructed persons who shall have made their first Communion.†

6. All priests of the O. C. R. must regard the Metropolitan Episcopal Chapter of the Catholic Church of England as authoritative in spiritual concerns. The Prelates of the Established Church (and of Churches in communion with it) can be recognized only as holding positions in which they represent the civil authority. Their Episcopal office, titles and spiritual functions cannot be regarded as possessing any real significance or efficacy, since their orders are not accepted as

valid in any portion of the Catholic Church, and their jurisdiction is derived from the State, or from persons lacking in power to confer spiritual jurisdiction.

  7. All priests of the O. C. R. are pledged to promote and extend the Holy Catholic Faith in its integrity, among their parishioners, and to assist the Catholic Church in England in every way that may be possible. There should be mutual co-operation between them and the clergy of the Catholic Church of England.

---

* The Society of St. Peter and St. Paul published a quasi-missal of this kind for the use of Anglican clergymen.

† See the vernacular "Missal and Ritual," published by Cope and Fenwich, 8, Buckingham Street, W.C., price 6s.

II.—FAITH.

The Mother of all Christian Churches is the Church of Jerusalem, founded upon the Feast of Pentecost, fifty days after the Ascension of our Lord Jesus Christ.

The choice of Apostles and the promotion of ecclesiastical dignities was made by election (Acts, i., 22-26 : vi., 3-6). Each Apostle received the plentitude of the Priesthood of Christ with all its powers, equally.

There is no evidence in Scripture or in primitive tradition that St. Peter, or his successors, were, or even intended to be, Supreme and Infallible Rulers or Despotic Monarchs in the Church. The Scriptures and early tradition and the Councils of the Church show that St. Peter and his successors were regarded as Primates among Equals and not as Despotic Monarchs nor as universal bishops. In addressing the College of the Apostles our Lord treated them as equals and bestowed equal powers upon them all (St. Matthew, xviii., 18 ; St. John, xx., 23 ; St. Matthew, xvi., 18, 19). The Faith of Jesus Christ is the Rock against which the storms of error and iniquity, and the hatreds and jealousies of sects, heresies and men will rage but ineffectually.

Upon this Faith and confession of the Apostles, expressed by Peter as their mouthpiece, the Church of God is built. There she remains, throughout the ages, unharmed, and the powers of darkness cannot prevail against her, because her foundation is secure.

The Catholic Church of England is so called for the following reasons: --

Firstly, she is Catholic because she believes and teaches everything held be the Universal Church and taught by her in all ages and places. Her Faith is that of the Primitive Church and she is consequently a part of the one divine Church, the Teacher of All Nations.

Secondly, the Catholic Church is the Church of all Nations. Of this Church the Catholic Church of England is a part. She holds the Faith as it was held by our Catholic forefathers from time immemorial. She comes to us as she came to our ancestors, and as she went from England to other nations, such as the ancient Frisians and the Teutons, proclaimed to the heathen by the Saints of old as the Ark of Man's Salvation. As the Catholic Church of England upholds the authority of the State, and teaches the duty and obedience to the law of the land, and of fidelity and loyalty to the Constitution.

The Catholic Church of England accepts the Creeds of the Universal Church, known as the Nicene, the Apostles' and the Athanasian Symbols. She does not recite the *Filioque* clause in the Creeds of Nicaea. In the administration of the Sacraments the Catholic Church of England uses exclusively the rites authorized, and of universal acceptance, in the Latin Church, contained in the liturgical works known as the *Rituale Romanum*, the *Missale Romanum* and the *Pontificale Romanum*. She permits the use of accurate translations of these works, where the vernacular is preferred and held to be desirable. At the same time preference should, as far as may be possible and expedient, be given to the generally used language of Western Christendom, which is Latin. All the ceremonies of the Church must be carefully carried out, without alternation or abridgment, wherever this may be possible. The rubrics of the Missal, Ritual, and Pontifical must be rigorously adhered to, unchanged.

No alterations in matters of Faith are permitted.

III. – DOGMATIC ARTICLES OF FAITH.

1. Eternal Salvation is promised to mankind only through the merits of our Saviour Jesus Christ, and upon condition of obedience to the teaching of the Gospel, which requires Faith, Hope and Charity, and the due observance of the ordinances of the Orthodox and Catholic Religion.

2. Faith is a virtue infused by God, whereby man accepts and believes without doubting, whatever God has revealed in the Church concerning true Religion.

Hope is a virtue infused by God, and following upon Faith; by it man puts his entire trust and confidence in the goodness and mercy of God, through Jesus Christ, and looks for the fulfillment of the Divine promises made to those who obey the Gospel.

Charity is a virtue infused by God, and likewise consequent upon Faith ; whereby man, loving God above all things for His own sake, and his neighbor as himself for God's sake, yields up his will to a joyful obedience to the revealed will of God in the Church.

3. God has established the Holy Catholic Church upon earth to be the pillar and ground of the revealed truth ; and has committed to her the guardianship of the sacred Scriptures, and of holy Tradition, and the power of binding and loosing.

4. The Catholic Church has set forth the principal Doctrines of the Christian Faith in twelve articles of the Creed, as follows:

I. I believe in one God the Father Almighty, Maker of heaven and earth, and of all things visible and invisible.

II. And in one Lord, Jesus Christ, the only-begotten Son of God, begotten of the Father before all worlds, God of God, Light of Light, True God of True God, begotten not made, of one substance with the he Father, by Whom all things were made.

III. Who for us men and for our salvation came down from heaven, and was Incarnate by the Holy Ghost of the Virgin Mary, and was made Man.

IV. And was crucified also for us under Pontius Pilate, He suffered and was buried.

V. And the third day He rose again, according to the Scriptures.

VI. And ascended into heaven, and sitteth on the right hand of the Father.

VII. And He shall come again, with glory, to judge the living and the dead; Whose kingdom shall have no end.

VIII. And in the Holy Ghost, the Lord, the Giver of Life, Who proceedeth from the Father; Who with the Father and the Son together is adored and glorified; Who spake by the Prophets.

IX. And in One, Holy, Catholic, and Apostolic Church.

X. I acknowledge one Baptism for the remission of sins.

XI. And I look for the resurrection of the dead.

XII. And the life of the world to come. Amen.

This sacred Creed is sufficient for the establishment of the Truth, inasmuch as it explicitly teaches the perfect Doctrine of the Father, the Son, and the Holy Ghost. As a symbol of Faith it is the summary or Creed of the three hundred and eighteen Fathers who met at Nicea in Bithynia, A.D. 325 ; it was completed and published by the authority of the Ecumenical Council of Constantinople, A.D. 381.

5. The fundamental ordinances of the Gospel, instituted by Jesus Christ as special means of conveying Divine Grace and influence to the souls of men, which are commonly called Mysteries or Sacraments, are Seven in number, namely: Baptism, Confirmation, the Holy Eucharist, Penance, Holy Orders, Holy Matrimony, and the Unction of the Sick or Extreme Unction.

(i.) Baptism is the first Sacrament of the Gospel, administered by threefold immersion in, or affusion with, water with the words, "I baptize thee" or "Let him be baptized," in the Name of the Father, and of the Son, and of the Holy Spirit." It admits the recipient into the Church, bestows upon him the forgiveness of sins, original and actual, through the Blood of Christ, and causes in him a spiritual change called regeneration. Without valid Baptism no other Sacrament can be validly received. Every person who received Baptism is thereby admitted into the Church of God.

(ii.) Confirmation or Chrism is a Sacrament in which the baptized person, on being anointed with Chrism consecrated by the Bishops of the Church, with the imposition of hands, receives the seal of the Gift of the Holy Ghost to strengthen him in the grace which he received at Baptism, making him a

strong and perfect Christian and a good soldier of Christ. In the West Bishops are the ordinary ministers of this Sacrament. In the East it is administered by the Priests.

(iii.) The Holy Eucharist is a Sacrament in which, under the appearance of Bread and Wine, the true and actual Body and Blood of Christ are given and received for the remission of sins, and unto everlasting life. After the prayer of Invocation of the Holy Ghost in the Divine Liturgy, the bread, and wine and water are entirely converted into the true, living and sacred Body and Blood of Christ by a real change of being to which change the philosophical term of transubstantiation is rightly applied. The celebration of this sublime Mystery constitutes the chief act of Christian worship, being a sacrificial Memorial of the Lord's death, and is called the Holy Mass. The Sacrifice is not a repetition of the Sacrifice once for all offered upon the Cross, but is a perpetuation of that Sacrifice upon the Earth, our Lord also perpetually offers it in heaven. Hence it is a true and propitiatory Sacrifice, which is offered for the living and the departed. Bishops and Priests alone are entitled to celebrate the Mass.

(iv.) Penance is a Sacrament, by which the Holy Ghost bestows the forgiveness of sins, by the ministry of the priest, on those who, having sinned mortally after Baptism, confess their sins with true repentance. The minister of Penance is the Priest or the Bishop.

(v.) Holy Orders is a Sacrament in which the Holy Ghost, through the laying-on of hands of Bishops, consecrates the pastors and ministers chosen by the Church, and imparts to them special grace to administer the Sacraments, and to feed the flock of Christ. The tonsure and the four minor orders precede reception of the major orders. Bishops alone have the power of conferring the Major or Holy Orders.

(vi.) Holy Matrimony is a Sacrament in which the voluntary union of husband and wife is sanctified to become an image of the union between Christ and His Church; and grace is imparted to them to fulfil the duties of their estate and its great responsibilities, both to one another and to their children. The ministers of this Sacrament are the contracting parties.

(*vii.*) Extreme Unction, or Unction of the Sick, is a Sacrament in which the Priests of the Church anoint the sick with oil for the healing of the infirmities of their souls, and, if it should please God, those of their bodies also. It is called "Extreme" because it is the last of the anointings given to Christian people, the first being at Baptism, the second at Confirmation, the third, in the case of clergy only, at their Ordination. Bishops and priests are the ministers of Extreme Unction.

The efficacy of the Sacraments depends upon the promise and appointment of God; howbeit they benefit those only who receive them worthily, with faith, and with a due preparation and disposition of mind.

6. Holy Scripture is given by the inspiration of God for the instruction and edification of His Church. The Books contained in the proto-Canon are the following: --

The Five Books of Moses.
Joshua.
Judges with Ruth.
Four Books of the Kings.
Two Books of Paralipomenon, or Chronicles.
Two Books of Esdras, called Ezra and Nehemias.
Esther.
Job.
The Psalter.
Proverbs, Ecclesiastes. The Canticle of Canticles.
Four greater Prophets.
Twelve Lesser Prophets.
All the Books of the New Testament.

The other Ecclesiastical Books of earlier date than those of the New Testament are not included in the Proto-Canon, but are Deutero-Canonical, and are accounted excellent, instructive and holy.

7. The Apostolical and Ecclesiastical Traditions received from the General Councils and the approved Fathers, may not be rejected, but are to be received and obeyed as being both agreeable to the Holy Scriptures and to God's Revelation. Matters of ceremonial and discipline are not on the same level with matters of faith, but are liable to variation.

8. There is a Communion of Saints in the Prayer of faith and love, and mutual union with Christ: wherefore it is pleasing to God,

and profitable to man, to honour His Blessed Mother, the Angels and the Saints, and to invoke them in prayer ; and also to pray for the Faithful Departed.

9. The relics and representations of the Saints are worthy of honour, as are also all other religious emblems, that our minds may be encouraged to devotion, and to imitation of the deeds of the just. The honor shown to such objects is purely relative.

10. It is the duty of all Christians to join in the Divine Worship ordered by the Church, *i.e.,* the Holy Sacrifice of the Mass, in accordance with Holy Tradition and to confirm to the ceremonies prescribed by her for the edification of the Faithful.

11. All Christians are bound to observe the Moral Law contained in the Ten Commandments of the Old Testament, developed with greater strictness in the New, founded upon the law of nature and charity, and defining our duty to God and to man. The laws of the Church are also to be obeyed, as proceeding from that authority which Christ has committed to her.

12. The Monastic Life, duly regulated according to the laws of the Church, is a salutary institution, in strict accord with Holy Scripture; and is full of profit to those who, being carefully tried and examined, make full proof of their calling thereto.

13. It is the duty of Christians to observe the penitential seasons, and the prescribed days of abstinence and fasting.

IV. – ORGANIC ARTICLES OF FAITH.

1. The Foundation Head and Supreme Pastor and Bishop of the Church is our Lord Jesus Christ Himself, from Whom all Bishops and Pastors derive their spiritual powers and jurisdiction.
2. By the laws and institution of our Lord Jesus Christ in the Gospel, all Christians owe obedience and submission in spiritual things to them who have rule and authority within the Church.
3. Our Saviour Jesus Christ hath not committed rule and authority in the Church to all the Faithful indiscriminately, but only to the Apostles and to their lawful successors in due order.
4. The only lawful successors of the Apostles are the Orthodox and Catholic Bishops, united by profession of the self-same belief and by participation in the same Sacraments. The Bishops of the Church, being true successors of the Apostles, are by Divine Right and appointment the rulers of the Church.

In virtue of this appointment, each individual Bishop is supreme and independent in that part of the Church which has been committed to his care, so long as he remains in Faith with the company of Catholic Bishops, who cannot exclude any from the Church except those who stray from the path of virtue or err in Faith. Heresy excludes from the Church *ipso facto.*

By virtue of this same Divine appointment, the supreme Authority over the whole Church on earth belongs to the collective Orthodox and Catholic Episcopate; they alone form the highest tribunal in spiritual matters, from whose united judgment there can be no appeal; so that it is unlawful for any single Bishop, or any number of Bishops, apart from them, or for any secular power or state, to usurp this authority; or for any individual Christian to substitute his own private judgment for that interpretation of Scripture which is approved by the Church.

5. The collective body of the Orthodox and Catholic Episcopate, united by profession of the Faith and by the Sacraments, is the source and depository of all order, authority and jurisdiction in the Church, and is the centre of visible Catholic unity.

The authority of this collective body is equally binding, however it may be expressed, whether by a General Council or by the regular and ordinary consultation and agreement of the Bishops themselves.

It is an act of schism to appeal from the known judgment of the Orthodox and Catholic Episcopate, however it may have been ascertained; or to appeal from any dogmatic decree of any General Council even though such appeal be to a future Council. For the Episcopate, being a continuation of the Apostolate, is clearly a Divine institution, and its authority is founded in Divine Right. Ecumenical Councils, as distinguished from all other means of ascertaining the common belief and judgment of the Episcopate are not of Divine appointment; and so the Episcopate having clearly the Scriptural promise of Divine guidance into all Truth, cannot be hampered in the exercise of its authority by the necessity of assembling a General Council which may obviously be rendered impossible through natural circumstances.

The authority of the Church can never be in abeyance, even though a General Council cannot be assembled; but it is equally to be submitted to and obeyed in whatever way it may be exercised, and although it be not exercised by means of a General Council, but by the universal consent of the Episcopate.

6. All Patriarchs, Archbishops, and Metropolitans without exception--that is to say, all Bishops who exercise any authority over other Bishops--owe that pre-eminence of authority solely to the appointment, or general consent of the Episcopate; and can never cease to owe obedience to the collective Body of the Episcopate in Council in matters concerning Faith and Morals.

7. There are five Patriarchates, which ought to be united and, with the Episcopate to form the supreme authority in governance of the Holy Catholic Church. These are Rome, Antioch, Alexandra, Constantinople, and Jerusalem. The Pope, as Patriarch of the West, and Bishop of Rome is Primate among Equals.

Unfortunately, owing to dispute and differences on the one hand, and to the lust for supremacy and domination on the other, the Patriarchs are not at present in union, and the welfare of Christendom is jeopardized by their disedifying quarrels, which, we pray, may cease. The government of the Church is constitutional and not despotic.

THE FIRST SEVEN ECUMENICAL COUNCILS.

The First Seven General Councils, recognized by the whole Catholic Church, *i.e.* in the East and in the West: area –
1. Nicea, A.D. 325, against Arianism
2. Constantinople, A.D. 381, against the Apollinarians and Macedonians.
3. Ephesus, A.D. 431, against Nestorianism.
4. Chalcedon, A.D. 451, against the Monophysites.
5. Constantinople, A.D. 553, against the Nestorians and the Monophysites.
6. Constantinople, A.D. 680, against the Monothelites.
7. Nicea, A.D. 787, against the Iconoclasts.

The Decrees of the Synod of Jerusalem, held under Dositheus in 1672, since they accurately express the belief and teaching of the Universal Church, are to be accepted as *de fide* by the Catholic Church of England.

The Catholic Church of England is in union with the Catholic Church of France, the Catholic Church of Ireland, the Catholic Church of North America, and the Catholic Church of Syria, and elsewhere.

Oath to be Subscribed by Candidates for Holy Orders.
=====================

To the Archbishop and Metropolitan of the London District.

+ In the name of the Holy and Undivided Trinity. – *Amen.*

I,..., having formally united with the Ancient Catholic Church of England, hereby declare that I know of no canonical impediment to my ordination, and that it is my firm purpose and intention, if ordained, to devote my life to the ministry of the Catholic Church of England; and I do hereby solemnly undertake and promise canonical obedience to the Archbishop and Metropolitan of the London District, and to all my ecclesiastical Superiors; and I promise that I will faithfully hold and teach without altercation the Faith of the Catholic Church of England which is that of the One Holy Catholic Apostolic and Orthodox Church, and is in accordance with the Decrees of the Holy Ecumenical Councils; and I hold an will hold the faith as it is defined, in precise terms, in the Nicaeno-Constantinopolitan Creed of the Universal Church and in the Definitions of the Ecumenical Councils.

I hereby profess my belief in the Holy Sacrifice of the Mass, in the Dogma of Transubstantiation, in the Seven Sacraments, and in the Decrees of the Synod of Jerusalem of 1672.

....
Date   *Witness:*

OATH TO BE SUBSCRIBED BY BISHOPS-ELECT BEFORE THEIR CONSECRATION.

TO THE ARCHBISHOP AND METROPOLITAN OF THE LONDON DISTRICT.

✠ *In the Name of the Father and of the Son and of the Holy Ghost. Amen.*

I,..., Bishop-elect of

... and now about to be consecrated by you, Most Reverend Father, by name

.., Archbishop of the London District, hereby profess and solemnly promise to you and to the Holy Metropolitan Church of London and to you successors in the said Church, canonically succeeding, due and canonical obedience, reverence and submission, to be shown by me at all times. And I will be the helper and loyal defender, maintainer and preserver of you the Archbishop

.... my Metropolitan, and of the said Church, according to my Order and power.

So help me God and these Holy Gospels of God. (HERE HE KISSES THE BOOK OF THE GOSPELS).

I,.., the aforesaid Bishop-elect, hereby subscribe and confirm the above with my own hand, before the Holy Altar

...

Bishop-elect of ....

...

Witness ....

Date...19............

TABLE OF APOSTOLIC SUCCESSION IN THE CATHOLIC CHURCH OF ENGLAND.

1. HIS EMINENCE ANTONIO CARDINAL BARBERINI, 1607-1671.

On August 30th, Pope Urban VIII, nominated his nephew, Antonio Barberini, aged 19, Grand Pior of the Order of the Knights of Malta at Rome and Cardinal of the Holy Roman Catholic Church. In Fisquet's *La France Pontificale* we fine the following facts concerning him recorded: --

Antonio Barberini was created Cardinal Deacon, receiving first the title of Santa Maria in Acquiro, which he exchanged a little later for that of Sant' Agatha della Suburra and Santa Maria in Via Lata. When he received ordination to the priesthood and promotion as Cardinal Priest, he took the title of Trinita dei Monti. In 1628 he became Legate in Avignon, in 1629 Legate *a latere* in Piedmont. In 1633 he was Charge' d' Affairs for matters concerning France and Rome, an appointment he held under Louis XIII for twelve years. In 1648 he was appointed Camerlengo of the Holy Church; and in 1641 he became Legate at Bologna, Ferrara, and in the Romagna; and in 1643 he was Generalissimo of the Forces of the Church opposing the League of Italian Princes, formed against the Barberini. On the 15th September, 1644, owing to the influence of the Barberini, Pope Innocent X ascended the Papal Throne, yet the Barberini had to quit Italy. By this time Cardinal Antonio Barberini has become powerful, and his relations took refuge, under his auspices, in France.

In 1652 Louis XIV issued a brevet nominating him Bishop of Portiers, but the Pope refused the bulls, although Cardinal Mazarin had reconciled Barberini to the Pontiff. King Louis XIV then appointed him Commander of the Order of the Holy Ghost and Grand Almoner of France. He took the Oath of Allegiance to the King on 28th April, 1653. In 1655 he took part on the Conclave which elected Fabio Chigi to the papacy, under the title of Alexander VII. IN 1655 he was consecrated Bishop of Frascati, in Rome. The consecrating prelate was Monsignore Scannarolo, Bishop of Sidonia, assisted by Monsignore Bottini, domestic Prelate of the Pope, and Laurenzio Gavotti, Bishop of Vintimiglia.

In 1657 Louis XIV nominated him Archbishop of Rheims, and in 1659, sent him as French Ambassador to the Holy See. In 1661 Cardinal Barberini was recognized as Bishop of Palestrina. His solemn entry and enthronement at Rheims took place on 22nd December 1667.

In 1668 he consecrated as his coadjutor, with right of succession, Monsigneur Le Tellier, and towards the close of the year 1669 he journeyed for the last time to Rome. He took up his abode at the Castle of Nemi, a few miles from Rome, where he died on the 3rd of August, 1671.

II. CHARLES MAURICE LE TELLIER, son of the Grand Chancellor of France, received the title of Archbishop of Nazianzen, *in partibus*, and later on succeeded Cardinal Barberini as Archbishop of Rheims. The consecration took place in the Church of the Sorbonne, at Parish, on 12th November, 1668. Archbishop le Tellier, by order of Pope Clement X, in the Church of the Cordeliers at Pontoise, consecrated on the 21st September, 1670---

III. JAMES BENIGNE BOSSUET, as Bishop of Condom, in the department of Gers. Boussuet was translated by Pope Clement X to Meaux, in 1671, and was ordered by the Pope to consecrate as his successor, in 1693, at the Church of the Chartreuse, Paris—

IV. JAMES GOYON DE MATIGNON, as Bishop of Condom. Bishop de Matignon, son of the Count of Thorigny, was Doyen of Liseux. He was appointed Bishop of Condom in 1671 and resigned his see after ruling the Diocese twenty years. He was also Abbe' Commendataire de St. Victor at Marseilles. He died at Paris 15th March, aged 84 years. By order of Pope Clement XI, Bishop de Matignon, on Quinquagesima Sunday, 12th February, 1719, consecrated at Paris, in the Chapel of the Fathers of the Foreign Missions—

V. DOMINIC MARY VARLET, as Bishop of Ascalon, *in partibus*, and coadjutor to Monseigneur Pidou de St. Olon, Bishop of Babylon, Persia. On the evening of his consecration Varlet received intelligence of the death of the Bishop of Babylon, whom he immediately succeeded to that see. Bishop Varlet, having incurred the Pope's displeasure by administering Confirmation in Holland, now retired to that country, where he resided with the Carthusian Fathers. He died twenty-three years later, in 1742, in the Cistercian Abbey at Rhijnwick. Bishop Varlet consecrated four Archbishops of Utrecht successively, the first three dying without conferring the episcopate. The fourth was consecrated 17th October, 1739, and was named—

VI. PETER JOHN MEINDAERTS, who died 3rd October 1767. Archbishop Meindaerts, who had been ordained priest by Luke Fagan, Bishop of Meath, afterwards Archbishop of Dublin was favourable to the Dutch Old Roman Catholics, on 11th July, 1745, consecrated as Bishop of Haarlem—

VII. JOHN VAN STIPHOUT, who died 16th December, 1777. Bishop van Stiphout consecrated as Archbishop of Utrecht on 7th February 1768—

VIII. WALTER MICHAEL VAN NIEUWENHUIZEN, who died 14th April, 1797 Archbishop van Nieuwenhuizen, on 21st June, 1778 consecrated as Bishop of Haarlem—

IV. ADRIAN BROCKMAN, who died in 1800. Bishop Brockman consecrated as Archbishop of Utrecht on 5th July, 179700

X. JOHN JAMES VAN RHIJN, who died in 1808. Archbishop van Rhijn consecrated as Bishop of Deventer, on 7th November, 1805—

XI. GISBERT DE JONG, who died in 1824. Bishop de Jong consecrated as Archbishop of Utrehct, on 24th April, 1814—

XII. WILLIBRORD VAN OS, who died in 1825. Bishop van Os, on 22nd April, 1819, consecrated as Bishop of Haarlem—

XIII. JOHN BON, who died in 1841. Bishop Bon, on 14th June, 1825, consecrated as Archbishop of Utrecht—

XIV. JOHN VAN SANTEN, who died in 1858. Archbishop van Santen, on 17 July, 1854, consecrated as Bishop of Deventer—

XV. HERMANN HEYKAMP, who died in 1874. Bishop Heykamp consecrated, on 11 August, 1873, as Bishop of Haarlem—

XVI. GASPARD JOHN RINKEL, who died in 1906. Bishop Rinkel, on 11th May, 1892, consecrated as Archbishop of Utrecht—

XVII. GERALD GUL, the present Archbishop (1914), who consecrated at Utrecht, on 28th April, 1908—

XVIII. ARNOLD HARRIS MATHEW, Bishop of Great Britain and Ireland, 1908; elected Archbishop and Metropolitan, 7th January, 1911.

XIX. On 7th January, 1911, Archbishop Mathew, in his domestic chapel at 151, Fellows Road, South Hampstead, consecrated—

FRANCIS BACON and CUTHBERT FRANCIS HINTON, and on 29th June, 1913, he consecrated—

THE PRINCE DE LANDAS BERGHES AND DE RACHE.

THE CATHOLIC CHURCH OF ENGLAND.

A PASTORAL LETTER ISSUED ON 29TH DECEMBER, 1910, BY ARCHBISHOP MATHEW.

DECLARATION OF AUTONOMY AND INDEPENDENCE.

We, the undersigned Bishop, on behalf of our clergy and laity of the Catholic Church of England, hereby proclaim and declare the autonomy and independence of our portion of the One, Holy, Catholic and Apostolic Church.

We are in no way whatever subject to or dependent upon any foreign See, nor do we recognize the right of any members of the religious bodies known as 'Old Catholics' on the Continent, to require submission from us to their authority or jurisdiction, or the decrees, decisions, rules or enactments of any of their Conventions, Synods, Congresses, or other assemblies, in which we have neither taken part nor expressed agreement.

The venerable Church of the Netherlands, which is a British and Irish foundation, due to the apostolic labours of St. Willibrord and St. Boniface, and consolidated by the efforts of other Saints and Monks of the ancient Churches of England and Ireland, remained staunch and true to its primitive Catholic belief, traditions and customs for more than twelve centuries.

With inexpressible joy, therefore, did we, in the year 1908 receive the sacred Episcopate, to be restored to our country through the instrumentality of His Grave the Most Reverend Lord Archbishop of Utrecht, Mgr. Gul, who presides over the small remnant of the ancient English Church still surviving in the Netherlands. Whilst retaining our profound respect for and gratitude to this estimable Prelate, we cannot but express the deep regret we feel that our hopes should have been disappointed in the way we now describe:

We had supposed and believed that the Faith, once delivered to the Saints, and set forth in the decrees of the Councils accepted as Ecumenical no less in the West than in the East, would have continued unimpaired, whether by augmentation or by diminution, in the venerable Church of the Dutch Nation.

We anticipated that the admirable fidelity with which the Bishops and Clergy of that Church had adhered to the Faith and handed it down, untarnished by heresy, notwithstanding grievous persecution during so many centuries, would never have wavered.

Unfortunately, however, we discover with dismay, pain, and regret that the standards of orthodoxy, laid down of old by the Fathers and Councils of the East and West alike, having been departed from in various particulars by certain sections of Old Catholicism, these departures, instead of being checked and repressed, are, at least tacitly, tolerated and acquiesced in without protest, by the Hierarchy of the Church of the Netherlands.

In order to avoid misapprehension, we here specify nine of the points of difference between Continental Old Catholics and ourselves:

(1) Although the Synod of Jerusalem, held under Dositheus in 1672, was not an Ecumenical Council, its decrees are accepted by the Holy Orthodox Church of the Orient as accurately expressing its belief, and are in harmony with the decrees of the Council of Trent on the dogmas of which they treat. We are in agreement with the Holy Orthodox Church, regarding this Synod, Hence, we hold and declare that there are Seven Holy Mysteries or Sacraments instituted by Our Divine Lord and Saviour Jesus Christ, therefore all of them necessary for the salvation of mankind, though all are not necessarily to be received by every individual, e.g. Holy Orders and Matrimony.

Certain sections, if not all, of the Old Catholic bodies, reject this belief and refuse to assent to the decrees of the Holy Synod of Jerusalem.

(2) Moreover, some of them have abolished the Sacrament of Penance by condemning and doing away with auricular confession; others actively discourage this salutary practice; others, again, whilst tolerating its use, declare the Sacrament of Penance to be merely optional, therefore unnecessary, and of no obligation, even for those who have fallen into mortal sin after Baptism.

(3) In accordance with the belief and practice Of the Universal Church, we adhere to the doctrine of the Communion of Saints by invoking and venerating the Blessed Virgin Mary, and those who have received the crown of glory in heaven, as well as the Holy Angels of God.

THE MOST REV. ARNOLD HARRIS MATHEW, *de jure* EARL OF LANDAFF,
FIRST ARCHBISHOP AND METROPOLITAN OF THE
CATHOLIC CHURCH OF ENGLAND.

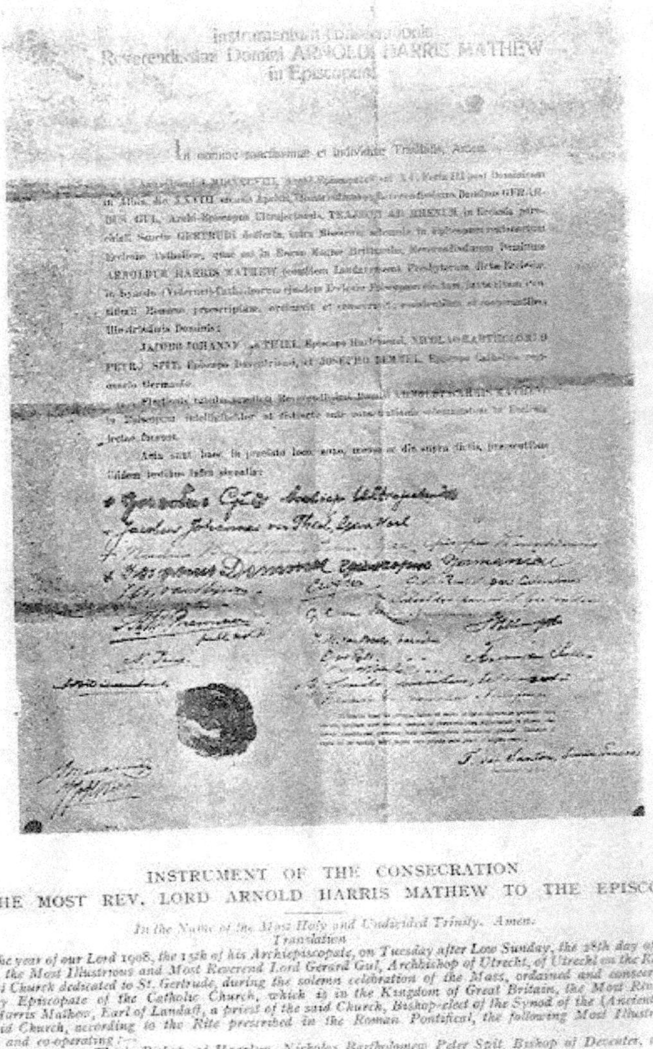
Instrumentum Consecrationis
Reverendissimi Domini ARNOLDI HARRIS MATHEW
in Episcopum

In nomine sanctissimae et individuae Trinitatis. Amen.

[illegible]

INSTRUMENT OF THE CONSECRATION OF THE MOST REV. LORD ARNOLD HARRIS MATHEW TO THE EPISCOPATE.

In the Name of the Most Holy and Undivided Trinity. Amen.

Translation

In the year of our Lord 1908, the 15th of his Archiepiscopate, on Tuesday after Low Sunday, the 28th day of the month of April, the Most Illustrious and Most Reverend Lord Gerard Gul, Archbishop of Utrecht, of Utrecht on the Rhine, in the Parochial Church dedicated to St. Gertrude, during the solemn celebration of the Mass, ordained and consecrated to the Regionary Episcopate of the Catholic Church, which is in the Kingdom of Great Britain, the Most Reverend Lord Arnold Harris Mathew, Earl of Landaff, a priest of the said Church, Bishop-elect of the Synod of the (Ancient) Catholics of the said Church, according to the Rite prescribed in the Roman Pontifical, the following Most Illustrious Lords assisting and co-operating :—

John James van Thiel, Bishop of Haarlem, Nicholas Bartholomew Peter Spit, Bishop of Deventer, and Joseph Demmel, Catholic Regionary Bishop of Germany.

The papers of the Election to the Episcopate of the said Most Reverend Lord Arnold Harris Mathew were intelligibly and distinctly read before the solemnity of the Consecration took place, in the Church.

These things were done in the aforesaid place, year, month and day above-stated, there being present the witnesses whose signatures appear as follows :—

Gerard Gul, Archbishop of Utrecht ;
James John van Thiel, Bishop of Haarlem ;
Nicholas Bartholomew Peter Spit, Bishop of Deventer ;
Joseph Demmel, Bishop of Germany.

J. W. Joan V. Leynes, T. L. W. H. Brammer, Notary Public, N. Prins, A. H. Deerenbach, S. J. W. ... (signature illegible), J. J. de Vries, C. Wyker, G. C. van Schaick, parish priest ; J. M. van Beek, parish priest ; G. V. D. Poll, parish priest ; P. W. Rinkel, parish priest ; B. Smit, parish priest of Utrecht ; F. Kenninck, parish priest of Amersfoort ; G. J. Rinkel, parish priest of Culemborg ; C. Deeder, parish priest of St. Gertrude's ; J. Pellemeyer, A. van der Poll.

And all these things were thus carried out and I testify that the above-written signatures are genuine and are those of the persons named, who also signed in my presence and many other persons of all conditions were present at this consecration.

That the which things may be truly and duly attested, I have signed with my own hand and sealed these with my seal.

T. VAN SANTEN,

The Old Catholics in the Netherlands have not yet altogether abandoned this pious and helpful custom, but, in some other countries, invocation of the Saints has been totally abolished by the Old Catholics. Even the Angelic Salutation, or *Ave Maria*, familiar to the lips of every Christian, is no longer recited by them, and from the various newly-devised vernacular liturgies, the names of the Saints have been omitted.

(4) Although it may be permissible and, indeed, very desirable, in some countries, and under certain circumstances, to render the Liturgy into the vernacular languages, we consider it to be neither expedient nor tolerable that individuals should compose new liturgies, according to their own particular views, or make alterations, omissions and changes in venerable rites to suit their peculiar fancies, prejudices or idiosyncrasies. We lament the mutilations of this kind which have occurred among the Old Catholics in several countries and regret that no two of the new liturgies composed and published by them are alike, either in form or in ceremony. In all of them the ancient rubrics have been set aside, and the ceremonies and symbolism with which the Sacred Mysteries of the Altar have been reverently environed for many centuries, have, either wholly or in part, been ruthlessly swept away. The Rite of Benediction of the Blessed Sacrament has also been almost universally abolished among the Old Catholics.

(5) Since the time of the Venerable Beade, "Old Rome," "the Imperial City," has always been regarded as the religious capital of Western Christendom, just as "new Rome" –Constantinople– became the religious capital of Eastern Christendom.

We, therefore, treading in the footsteps of our Catholic forefathers, and in accordance with the decrees of the Ecumenical Councils, regard the Bishop of Old Rome as Primate of Christendom and as Patriarch of the West, and our desire is to exhibit due respect and veneration of the person of His Holiness in that exalted station.

In accordance with the primitive teaching of the Church of the Netherlands, which prevailed until a very recent date, we consider it a duty on the part of Western Christians to remember His Holiness the Pope as their Patriarch in their prayers and sacrifices. The name of His Holiness should, therefore, retain its position in the Canon of the Mass, where, as we observed at our consecration in Utrecht, it was customary, and remained so until a recent date in the present year (1910), for the celebrant to recite the name of our Patriarch in the usual manner in the Mass and in the Litany of the Saints. The publication of a new vernacular Dutch Liturgy in the present year causes us to regret that the clergy of Holland are now required to omit the name of His Holiness in the Canon of the Mass. Happily, only a small number of other alterations in the text of the Canon have, so far, been introduced. These, however, include the audible recitation of the whole of the secret prayers of the Mass, and the omission of the prayer *Haec Commixtio*, also the omission of the title, 'ever Virgin' whenever it occurs in the Latin Missal.

Such alterations pave the way for others of an even more serious nature, which may be made in the future, and, as we think, are to be deplored.

Among other sections of Old Catholicism not only have all public prayers for the Western Patriarch been abandoned, but the historical position and legitimate and generally-recognized prerogatives of His Holiness have been ignored, whilst, by some, a tone of bitterness and vulgar insolence has been introduced in referring to the Roman Pontiff, which is only comparable to that adopted by the most vituperative, ignorant and inveterate of the Protestant sects. This attitude we deeply regret and entirely disassociate ourselves from it. *Caritas benigna est.*

(6) Following the example of our Catholic forefathers, we venerate the adorable Sacrifice of the Mass as the supreme act of Christian worship instituted by Christ Himself. We grieve that the Old Catholic clergy, in most countries, have abandoned the daily celebration of Mass, and now limit the offering the Christian Sacrifice to Sundays and a few of the greater Feasts.

The corresponding neglect of the Blessed Sacrament, and infrequency of Holy Communion, on the part of the laity, are marked.

(7) In accordance with Catholic custom and with the decrees of the Ecumenical Councils, we hold that the honor and glory of God are promoted and increased by the devout and religious use of holy pictures, statues, symbols, relics, and the like, as aids to devotion, and that, in relations to those they represent, they are to be held in veneration. The Old Catholics have, generally speaking, preferred to dispense with such helps to piety.

(8) We consider that the Holy Sacraments should be administered only to those who are members of the Holy Catholic Church, not only by Baptism, but by the profession of the Catholic Faith in its integrity, by repudiation of all heresies, by rejection of any bond of union, and refusal of actual communion, with all persons and sects professing unorthodox beliefs, whether as individuals, or by formularies to which they are committed. Unhappily, we find persons who are not Catholics are now admitted to receive Holy Communion in all Old Catholic places of worship on the Continent. Although Communion under one species is still regarded as sufficient, non-Catholics desiring Communion under both species are communicated, out of deference to their tenants.

Moreover, clergymen of the Anglican Communion, whose Orders are open to the gravest doubt, have been permitted to celebrate the "Service for the Administration of Holy Communion," from the Anglican book of devotion, entitled "The Book of Common Prayer," at old Catholic altars, thus causing both Catholics and Protestants to suppose that Anglican Orders are accepted as valid by the Old Catholics in general.

(9) The Old Catholics have ceased to observe the prescribed days of fasting and abstinence, and no longer observe the custom of receiving Holy Communion fasting.

For these and other reasons, which it is unnecessary to detail, we, the undersigned Bishop, desire, by these presents, to declare our autonomy and our independence of all foreign interference in our doctrine, discipline and policy. *In necessaries unites, in dubiis libertes, in omnibus caritas.*

Given under our hand and sealed with our seal on this 29th day of December, the Feast of St. Thomas of Canterbury, in the year of our Lord one thousand nine hundred and ten.*
+Arnold Harris Mathew

A few slight alterations have been made in this pastoral letter.

WHAT IS MEANT BY THE CATHOLIC CHURCH OF ENGLAND?

1. The Catholic Church is a visible society composed of all human beings, who have received admission into it by a rite called Baptism.

2. Membership of the Baptized in the visible Church is retained by the profession of the Faith, revealed by God and made known to man by the teaching voice of the Church, *i.e.*, the Episcopate. The members of the Church are divided into two classes, namely, the Church teaching and the Church taught. It is the duty of the teaching church to make known to all mankind what it is that God has revealed, and therefore wishes to be believed concerning Himself, and concerning the origin and the destiny of the human soul.

3. The Catholic Church sets before man his duty — to God, to his neighbour and to himself — in the Creeds ; in the Decrees of the Ecumenical Councils ; in the Precepts of the Decalogue ; in the Commandments of the Church ; in the Scriptures, and in their Exposition by the Fathers and by learned theologians ; and in the universally accepted Catholic tradition.

4. The Catholic Church assists mankind to observe the Divine and Ecclesiastical Laws ; to live in union with God the Universal Spirit ; and, to prepare for immortality after the death of the Body. This it does by teaching the nature, value and manner of prayer, adoration and worship, and by opening to all men the seven mystical channels through which grace flows from God to the Soul, these channels being the seven Holy Sacraments, instituted by God.

5. The Divine Church is recognized by her four distinguishing marks or notes, viz : 1. She is One in Faith, Sacraments, and the Sacrifice of the Mass ; 2. She is Holy, in doctrine, and in presenting the means of sanctification to all men ; 3. She is Catholic, in belonging to all ages and to all nations ; 4. She is Apostolic in possessing the Apostolic ministry instituted by God Himself, and perpetuated by succession and ordination in the Church. Apart from the Apostolic Ministry the society called "the Church" could not exist.

6. The Catholic Church of England is so-called because she is identical in Faith, Sacraments, Sacrifice, and Apostolic ministry with the rest of the One Holy Catholic Apostolic Church of all the ages, and of all the world, from the days of the holy Apostles onwards.

THE MOST REV. GERASSIMOS MESSARRA,
The Prince Archbishop of Beirut, Syria, in the Patriarchate
of Antioch, who, on 5th August, 1911, received Archbishop
Mathew, and with him the Bishops, Clergy and Faithful
of the Catholic Church of England, into union with the
Orthodox Church.
The Arabic handwriting and signature above the portrait
and the French signature and inscription below it are in
Mgr. Messarra's own handwriting.

As a part of Catholic Christendom located in England, she is intended for the help, benefit, consolation and salvation of the inhabitants of England ; therefore she is the real, authoritative, primitive and true Catholic Church of England.

She is also the "Old" Church of England because she teaches only the Faith of Old England, as it was taught when our forefathers all believe alike and worshipped together, and before any religious disputes, sects and religious differences among Christians existed in this country.

The Catholic Church of England desires now to unite all Englishmen once more in acceptance and practice of the Old Religion of England, as it was for 1,000 years before the foreign novelties of the German and Swiss "Reformers" in the sixteenth century were introduced into our country. The Catholic Church of England is called "Western" and "Orthodox" because she is Orthodox in her teaching and situated in the West. The Catholic Church of England is also "Old Roman," because she is within the Patriarchate of Old Rome, just as the Catholic Church of the Levant is within the Patriarchate of New Rome. This name, "New Rome," was given to the City of Constantinople when the Emperor removed his Court from the old Imperial City on the Tiber to the New Imperial City on the Bosphorus.

7. The Catholic Church of England hopes to establish the church in many other countries, in each of which it will be autonomous, in accordance with the constitution of the Church in the early ages in the West, and that of the Church of the present day (which remains unchanged), in the East.

8. The Catholic Church of England resists despotism and tyranny in any part of the Church, as being of purely human invention, injurious no less to despots, tyrants and autocrats than to those who are victims of their domination, ambition or superstition.

9. The Catholic Church of England will, with all its might, endeavour to repress all ecclesiastical abuses, whether of authority or arising out of exaggeration, misapprehension, love of domination, imagination, fable, imposture, legend, or whatever cause.

The Revelation of God is one, and must be accepted as He has revealed it, without diminution or addition or altercation.

10. To teach or act in opposition or hostility to the Catholic Church of England, or to its lawfully constituted Hierarchy, is an act

of schism. To teach and act in unison with it, is lawful and well-pleasing to God. "He that gathereth not with Me Scattereth." (St. Luke xi., 23). To deny any article of the Catholic Faith, held and taught everywhere by the Universal Church, is an act of heresy, *which excludes from the pale of the Church.*

11. Those persons, however, who do not know or understand, and who have no means or opportunity of knowing, or possess no ability to understand the Faith of the Catholic Church are nevertheless invisibly united to what is spoken of as "the soul" of God's Church, and are thus in the way of Salvation, provided they act up to the light that is in them and obey the dictates of their consciences with fidelity. Hence, no man is excluded from the eternal life of the soul in bliss, excepting through his own fault. With increase of knowledge there is a corresponding increase of responsibility. We must remember that Almighty God is infinite in all Perfections, and among these are Justice and Truth as well as Mercy.

NOW THIS IS ETERNAL LIFE : THAT THEY MAY KNOW THEE, THE ONLY TRUE GOD, AND JESUS CHRIST WHOM THOU HAST SENT. (St. John xvii., 3.)

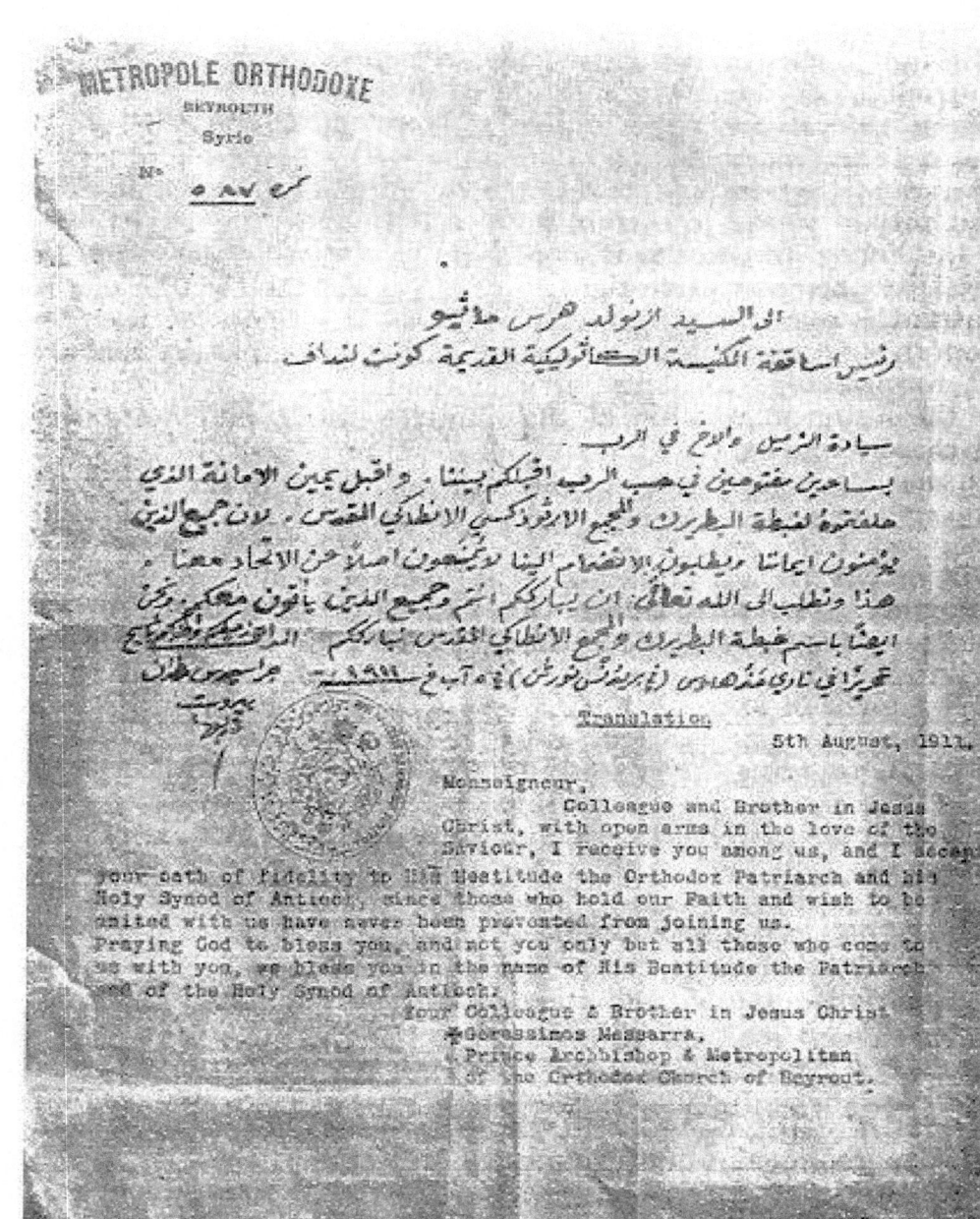

ARABIC CERTIFICATE OF THE RECEPTION OF THE CATHOLIC CHURCH OF ENGLAND INTO UNION WITH THE ORTHODOX EASTERN CHURCH.

SUMMARY OF THE FAITH AND THE AIMS OF THE CATHOLIC CHURCH OF ENGLAND.

Our differences with the Italian Curia are chiefly disciplinary and administrative. We aim, not at disunion or at reformation, but at reconstruction, on canonical and constitutional lines. We object to the centralization of all authority in the person of a single Patriarch. Our aim is *(a)* restore their ancient rights and privileges of authority — (i.) to each of the five Patriarchs, the first of whom is the Pope ; (ii.) to the Bishops ; *(b)* to restore to the clergy and laity their primitive right to take part in the election of their Patriarchs and Bishops ; *(c)* to liberate the clergy of the West from the unnatural and injurious obligation of compulsory celibacy ; *(d)* to encourage the laity to value and take an intelligent part in the liturgical worship of the Church ; *(e)* to promote a spirit of charity among Christians of all denominations ; to repress all sentiments of bitterness and fanaticism; to accentuate all points of agreement with others, and to minimize, as far as possible, points of disagreement, with a view that he accomplishment of the Will of our Divine Lord, that His followers should be united in one body. *(St. John,* xvii.) Our wish is to assist in every pious effort to re-unite the Eastern Orthodox and the Western Churches, and to bring into Catholic unity and communion all men and women of good-will of other denominations, who may care to help us in our work of evangelization, which is based upon the two precepts of our Lord Jesus Christ — (i.) "Thou shalt love the Lord thy God with all thy heart, and with all thy mind, and with all thy strength" ; (ii.) "Thou shalt love thy neighbour as thyself." We do not condemn, nor find fault with, those who conscientiously differ from us. We offer the right hand of fellowship to all, regardless of religions, national, or racial differences.

Our Faith is based upon the Apostolic Tradition, the Nicaeno-Constantinopolitan Creed, the Definitions of the Ecumenical Councils, and the teachings of the Holy Scriptures and the Fathers.

The *Filioque* clause is omitted from the Nicene Creed by the Orthodox Eastern Church, by the Melchite Greek, and by other Oriental Uniates, unified with the Roman See, and by ourselves.

Our ceremonies and liturgical vestments are those of Western Christendom.

We acknowledge the decrees of the Synod of Jerusalem of 1672, prescribing belief as *de fide* in Seven Sacraments instituted by our Lord Jesus Christ, in the Holy Sacrifice of the Mass and in Transubstantiation.,

We practice:--Veneration and Invocation of the Glorious and Immaculate Mother of God, ever Virgin, of the Angels and of the Saints ; prayers for the Faithful Departed ; the use of religious pictures, statues and symbols, as aids to faith and devotion ; and the Veneration of Sacred Relics. The formation of Religious Orders is included in our scheme of reconstruction. We recognize the ancient Patriarchates of Rome, Antioch, Jerusalem, Alexandria and Constantinople, and desire the re-union, co-operation and mutual recognition of their Holinesses, the five Patriarchs. Since God Himself is Truth and the Author of all Truths, we believe that scientific truth and spiritual truth must always be in harmony and that collision or conflict between them is impossible. Neither can true religion be harmed or its progress impeded by bold, honest, straightforward enunciation of scientific, historical, or theological ascertained facts, nor can true religion be assisted by fraud, falsehood, consceilment of the truth, exaggeration, or any kind of imposture. We abhor simony and decline to accept any earthly reward in return for any sacraments or spiritual graces received from us.

=====================

EXTRACT FROM A LETTER FROM HIS HOLINESS PHOTIOS, POPE AND PATRIRIARCH OF THE ORTHODOX CHURCH OF ALEXANDRIA, TO ARHBISHOP MATHEW.

To   Monsigneur Arnold Harris Mathew, Archbishop and Metropolitan (of the Catholic Church of Englad) of Londom, Earl of Landaff.

Health and salvation in our Lord   .   . We are very happy to announce to you that we have thanked God our Saviour for your categorical declarations that you regard the Pope of Rome as the first of the Patriarchs of Christianity, without, however, recognizing in him greater rights than the Orthodox Church acknolwledges, that you omit the *Filioque* clause, and that you do not accept money for celebrating Masses.

We agree with you as to the observance of you autonomy, and of the Latin rite in actual use, so long and so far as they agree with the Holy Dogmas and with the canonical ordinances of the Seven Ecumenical Councils, which form on the basis of the Orthodox Faith. On this basis we shall, with pleasure, facilitate arrangements with you, or with your Emissaries, this basis having no other foundation that which has been laid, Who is Jesus Christ; and with a good heart and in joy we glorify the Divine Grace and Power.

We embrace you and we enfold you in our arms in fraternal love in the one only Savior, in one only faith, in one only Baptism, in one only God and Father of all, Who is above all and through all and in us all.

As may our Father in Heaven, the God of peace, Who has raised from the dead the great Pastor of the Sheep, our Saviour Jesus, accomplish in you, in every fashion, all good works in accordance with His Will. May He perform in us that which is pleasing to him through Jesus Christ, to Whom be the glory forever and ever. And may we be made perfect in Jesus Christ, Amen.

Alexandira, the 13-26 February, 1912.

The Pope and Patriarch of Alexandria,

+ PHOTIOS.

DESIGN FOR THE CATHEDRAL OF OUR LADY OF ENGLAND.

THE CATHEDRAL WE DESIRE TO BUILD FOR THE CATHOLIC CHURCH OF ENGLAND, AS ITS METROPOLITAN CHURCH. £175,000 REQUIRED.

"Who can enter the western doorway of a French or an English cathedral without being immediately struck with religious awe? Not only at Chartres, but at Ely, Lincoln, Winchester, York and many other cathedrals in England the same description of glorious Gothic, the same wonderment at the science and glory of ecclesiastical architecture, fills one with some unaccountable sensation of which no other structure induces. And I venture so far as to say that no "classic" ecclesiastical structure affects one to anything like the same degree. A Gothic cathedral conveys, to my mind, a divine inspiration; it soaring vault; the marvellously delicate points of support; its varied shadows; its inexpressible beautiful pose, and its gathering together in one charming whole all the arts and sciences with music and oratory as culminating glories."

WM. WOODWARD, F.R.I.B.A.
(*The Observer*, 17 May, 1914)

Church Row, Hampstead, May 15.

Printed at the office of "The Bromley Chronicle," Sherman Road, Bromley, Kent.